Never Mind

June 6, 2018

Christine -
with best wishes

Katherine

Never Mind

Katherine Lawrence

TURNSTONE PRESS

Never Mind
copyright © Katherine Lawrence 2016

Turnstone Press
Artspace Building
206-100 Arthur Street
Winnipeg, MB
R3B 1H3 Canada
www.TurnstonePress.com

Turnstone Press gratefully acknowledges the assistance of the Canada Council for the Arts, the Manitoba Arts Council, the Government of Canada through the Canada Book Fund, and the Province of Manitoba through the Book Publishing Tax Credit and the Book Publisher Marketing Assistance Program.

Printed and bound in Canada by Friesens for Turnstone Press.

Library and Archives Canada Cataloguing in Publication

Lawrence, Katherine, 1955-, author
        Never mind / Katherine Lawrence.

Poems.
Issued in print and electronic formats.
ISBN 978-0-88801-559-4 (hardback).--ISBN 978-0-88801-561-7 (mobi).--ISBN 978-0-88801-560-0 (epub)

        I. Title.

PS8573.A91135N48 2016   C811'.6   C2016-901721-4
                                                 C2016-901722-2

In memory,
Helen Marion O'Hanley
(July 6, 1928 – April 1, 2011)

Contents

I Must Not Let the Fire Grow Hysterical

The Oxen Dialogues

Artist Unknown

Never Mind

Prologue

Under my Fingernails: Sand, Clay, Oxide of Iron

Down we go, down through the centuries, past maps, ships
& telescopes, past tents, wagons & muskets, past threadbare
rugs, cracked ceilings & water-stained walls, past iron
pots, cook-stoves, china cups & plates, past silver spoons,
wooden spoons, tea & whiskey, mullioned windows, tulip
wallpaper, past charcoal drawings, oxen, chickens, sheep,
furs & velvet collars, past children's leggings, orange-
yoked eggs, clay pipes, rail lines, iron beds & pine cradles,
past gardeners in black macintosh coats digging graves
in the rain, past chimneys, fire, ashes & honey-coloured
hearthstone, heart:stone
down
we go,
down.

Lit with Cunning

how many women unbalanc'd from their orbit fly?

In a Manner Particular to the Stitch Fallen

Did as I was bid:
stripped to smallclothes

in a parlour furnished with All necessary
sewing trestle, thread & cutting blades—

stood statuary while Mother draped
over my head muslin yardage

white as her face rising
above the horizon of folds,

a pale moon pocked with pins.
She basted sleeves in wide mimic

of wings, cloud-puffed the shoulders,
pinched, tucked, righted me ready,

her hand to steady as I gathered
raw hems & stepped from cold

speckled-stone floor to table top,
slow-turned my feet, hips, spine

my length laddered—
trembling at the view of marriage.

The Swell & Pitch of the Surging Grief

In the stale hold of a sailing ship I am Wife
sickly bedded & aflame.

He mutters *Love.* I name it *ship's fever,* toss
the meager contents of my soup stomach
into a bucket filled with the foul slop of Fortune:

babies born, babies lost, babies gone—
pound notes converted to backwoods so far
inland I fail, I never—
my mother, my sisters
the smell of salt brine, fingertips lipped with fog,
—ever again.

From this hold my New World fears climb ashore
while I remain on board, knees hugged to chest.

Taverns outnumber churches,
whisky divides the Lady who paints:
        watercolour wildings—
        daisies in their final stages of consumption,
        fever red roses,
        pitcher plant native to bog & swamp.

I seek counsel, ask my husband
does he worry our future, smell the wrong
in black smoke flagging the shore.

I need Chill air, the upper deck, arms agreeable strong.
We must ready about, helm's-a-lee, *sine qua non*
but he squares his brace. I grip the rail.

I will remember his breath down my collar back,
the slap of wind as I turn my face.

In Rubble

Dear Captain—,
Cupped my heart of hearts in newsprint. Did crate
& Nest my treasures as advised
      : glass sugar & creamer
      : paint pots
      : blue crockery tea set
      : porcelain vase.

I wish to report the promise shattered
my worldly reduced to fragments, slivers, Sir—

In your experience the world over & vast,
how does one repair the ruined vessel?

At the Heart of a Cedar Swamp

What brought me here—four walls of stacked logs, a roof
that leaks frost & clinging small clusters of mud stars—
what brought me here—

Reduced to such economy of means that I cross-write
between lines dried & previously committed, pledge

       my pen to space white unmarked, unsealed or
rendered readable by the tender unfolding of a corner,
a spare edge—

Such is my great dissimilarity to man's idea of Clearing: the
felling axe, a glory blaze criminal.

What brought me here—
I sit with little comfort on a slat-back chair before a writing
table that wobbles under the press of my hand, wax taper,

bit of paper & the company of Forest
unsympathetic in its grand Surround: these pines
do not pine
no boughs cradle

nothing weeps, nor leans in my direction

but wind.

I Am Unreposed & Wanting

If a ship had wings.
If the expanse of oceans. Distance
the collapse of shores. I would have sailed home to attend,
smart-stepped, disembarked, chin up.
In honour of you.
Mother—

        Nightmares of horse & hearse in a blacking mass.
Trumpeters ring my ears, penetrate
cotton wool, gloved hands, pillows, quilts.

If I had learned the lessons of map & compass,
how to change direction, wrestle a barrel-chested captain
for the helm   if I had listened to you
If your cough—or your thin chest.

Dear Mother,
Your letter arrived this morning. So good to learn the boys
are helping manage the shop & that Dr. L—believes you have
the strongest constitution in all of England. I trust you take
strength from your brushes & paints, that a Sunday might
find you & your easel among the hills beyond a shivering
wind. I might scope you more easily from my side of the
Atlantic if I knew, if I had only known, your palette held a
pigment of sun. Your hair fixed plain, a canvas apron tied
tight as my will to stand the distance & fix you in my gaze.
Forever—

Neither in these Fields

Do you believe?
Is it? A better land? I reference not Canada—
not this single room on the edge
of collapse—
       I speak of the far afield away—

       Sister: Do you imagine her in another Extreme?
I confess to covetous fits that you remain in walking close.
That you build a pretty
architecture for your visits graveside: red plaid throw,
seed-cake baked
by the hands of her favourite:
                Caraway seeds
                Butter
                Flour
            Three eggs fresh
         Sugar, a splash of milk
       (I was once her pet. Not you.)

Was it the Lungs that took her?
A sudden mortification of the brain?

I fear I have it backwards in these backwoods: my stove
crouches cold,
soup pot rests in want of potatoes, carrots, Yours & Truly,
a bit of beef,
something to feed this grief.

13

Rook's Feather Marks her Splendor

Parceled, boxed & posted
across time.

Stitch-bound paper
hard black cover
wider than its height.

What else?

Horsehair brushes, pencils, charcoal,
fine nibs, broad reed pens.

Paints, inks—all mother's, all mine:
yellow ochre,
raw sienna,
India red,
crimson lake,
purple madder,
lamp black

zinc white for clouding pigment
not memory.

Her eyesight turned storm, her pen & brush
a lightning strike.

Yet she observed, sketched
the collapse of days, years—
a rook's feather pressed between pages.

I follow her lead.

Sketch, journal, paint, record
without heed as years flare, burn & drop
from sky to grave.

Pocketbook Memorandum
Sketch (i)

Flickertail of green light as his eyes made great show of
presenting me with a plant named Jack. Marry me, he said.
We've a preacher. Did my brush not blush?

Hooded purple-brown
Jack-in-the-Pulpit
Indian turnip, bog onion
root-sundered & vased
in a peat stump.

Peace Offering
Ink Wash on Note Page

Pocketbook Memorandum
Sketch (ii)

On this day of never-rest, he grew for me a bedside orchard in our single room.

White hymnal
crossed the ocean,
came to rest
atop a wooden
apple box,
blossomed
& turned
pink.

Hymned & Crated
Watercolour on Note Page

Pocketbook Memorandum
Sketch (iii)

Something in the half-sleep rouses me to domestic troubles in the far away but Husband hushes me so loving-tight I soon let drift all worry.

Wild parsnip
wild cherry
wild tansy
wild honey
wild goose
wild roadstead
wild fire
wild winds
wild passions
grown wild.

Wildered
Pencil on Note Page

Pocketbook Memorandum
Sketch (iv)

His hands are candle-holders as I pace the dark. He lights the
tallow for my paints, shadows me until I curtain.

Standing trees timbered
house beams & rafters
boards, planks
hewed, sawed & launched—
mast pole for chimney
white gingham sails
captain in navy dress

the compass eyes of a lady.

Land-Locked
Watercolour on Note Page

Marriage Be Intimacies Scarce Imagined

I confide you in the enterprise of fluids viscous &
discharged slick for want of what these woods will have me
bring forth—mink, muskrat, fox? His seed tunnels dank
terrain before nesting heavy spent.

In the After, we wipe ourselves of musk but he
forgets his London manners & rushes first
for washwater heated
tepid & intended for my small parts not
his neck mouth eyes   towel hangs grim, puddles sweat
the floor where his boots
track hither & beyond.

Sister, I digress,
I covet two drops oil of Lavender—
such trouble to perform a morning task simple: Look
how I straddle thus & so above a porcelain
basin, sponge water the colour of tea gone cold—

I remain—
Damp & Uneven clean.

Wood Shack Furnished with a Ceiling that Drips Sudden Thaw

Shrink his woolen socks? He'll work barefoot in his boots.
Scorch his shirt? He'll pet the pony-smooth patches of shine.

Set flame to chair rockers? He'll seat his haunches on a milking
stool, resume mute calculations in rhythm unbroken.

I hate his silence.

Poison the soup? He'll ask for more broth.
Axe his wrists at the cuff? He'll sleeve a line of sweat from
his brow. Rope & twist at the Adam's apple?
He'll swallow honey soothing from a buzzing hive.

I dare look & see his gaze studded with nails & hammer.
He is obdurate as a stone mule.

dear me,
I awoke this December day to black tar paper fixed to
windows, frost-caked, cracked, the room thick with gloom.
Where once was ivy green imagined, tendrils clawed &
clinging to the memory of childhood skipping down the front
path, cardinal feather stemmed fancy in my hat band—

How he has swallowed the Very sun.
I remain, Lit with cunning.

Keepsake of Affection Pinned Miniature Close

Oval portrait pierced to my flannel dress:
watercolour & brown wash on ivory.
Father framed in sunlight. Here

on the verso, his black Curl whorled under glass.
Mother supposed
                I keepsake him by heart & so

I fasten thus, left of crux, yet all
I stock of him is pipe tincture. Come darkness
                          I unpin his stare,
                          prepare my undress
trace a jeweler's black pouch for essence
of her touch smooth
the leather worn. She brooched
                him daily, slipped him nightly

                keen to join   again.

How his gaze is fixed to her star.

In a Forest of Frost, a Dawn of Coneflowers

I ignore the hiss from Villager lips.
They say my hair is a bird's nest toppled.

My shape, the hourglass.
I fear I am too pretty.

They name me Fool for my vague unknowing to milk
a goat, rise bread from a dead stove, heel & toe the ice & snow.

How they divine my ruin.

But for wood violet, trillium, the Canadian rose
I would be haunted for want of talk.
      Who knocks? Maple leaves reddened with gossip—
                Come in—

Already the Light Is Slipping

We couple in the manner of trapped game.
He snares.
I thrash.

                                  He promises.
This time will be quick: arms above head, wrists tied
tight: reef knot, sailor's knot; I dare-move-not.

Ankles—

Someone opined (too late):
Never marry a soldier trained in the patient learning
of rope.

My log house is a barrack decorated in the palette of rabbit:

Grey mattress on a dirt floor.
White frost hoaring the window.
Buff shadows crouched in corners.
Red for the spill of light dying.

It Is Wondrous what Mischief these Morsels of Creation Can Do

Holes in my bunting dress, holes in the carded wool
gifted me by Mrs V—I had never worn but thrice.

How now I am fashion's Imperfect shot through, peepshow
eyelet patches of sin I'll not bother to confess.

My state of undress, half-dress, rip & tear torn
sleeves, unseemly to all but the palest grey

moths, their powdered hail dusting my costume.
I am outfitted in a manner Botanical. I am

the latest trend: Black eyes blind-stitched,
collar beaded & chewed. Soon I will stroll

the dark, sleep away the shine.

Making Dew

Among the Collects of this day, a reed-thin leaf green
                              grinning with drops Precious
                              crushed for my toilette.

                              I tip & Dab underside:
                              behind my ears, wrists,
                              back of knees.

                              Scent reminiscent
                              ocean swell, white mist.

The Days Are Brief & Pale, the Nights
Deep Lakes Dark

I have dwelt upon the circumstances of a January night:
moon curtained its face. And in the moment Very
his rough prowled hard & burrowed the hollow.

       By morning brief I was a bruised bank of cloud.

Now this—a thing akin,
tiny fingers & toes, the accretion of nails—
eyes lidless & starved for measure.

I blink not. Or sudden move lest I unrest the fetal heel & fist
of civil war.

       Cupid, you are stupid,
       we are friends no more.

I request a Greater attendance: midwife witch angel stranger
neighbour
beggar squaw.

How I fear the hour, how
Other will snake the lake-dark length of me—

Help Boiled the Kettle Scalding & Found a Twice Tied Bit of Twine

Night stopped me dumb.
I was rush & trembling cold,

lit inside out, bent double-fisted & Swamped,
smell of animal essence abed—

I was lightning sheets & bolt, oak split-thrashed
& heaving black shadows, buckled unwomanly

hideous, squatted round & down, pushed
hard-to-lee against a rising blood-swell, pitched

splayed ribbed open—   Help

tucked a creature in the Crook of my arm,
its tiny face a rictus of storm.

A second Other
duplicate small, shown Proof to me,

arranged in a basket pillowed
with dead leaves, violet-veined.

The Species I Hold Sucks Monstrous Delicate

Arrows of pain sharp as the pin bones of gutted salmon
dive the lady parts of me, pierce
my breasts, leave ache where once I was girl
at home in a room decorated with framed
flowers, watercolour blossoms
each stem cut from a different season I believed
perennial Evermore.

I want roses lilacs tulips purple asters peonies
scissored & delivered to me for me from—

I want chimney sweep to broom this room of atmosphere
maternus.

I want nurse in starched stark whites to lift this creature up,
up, & godspeed her
                    to the lie of a floral still life.

Dear me—fluids river the declivities of my descent, run
ribboned pink with blood streaked bright
as the lining of this creature's throat—

Where Am I Become?

In my bold answer to his blue eyes,
I turned sheep by virtue of a gold ring.

Canada mania & the brass agent
who recruited our crossing.

I regret: the stillborn &
rank smells clinging slick.

Pocketbook Memorandum
Sketch (v)

In slumber close'd her silver-streaming eyes.

Pine drawer lined
with spoons,
shallow bowls nested
inside the pale lustre
of the next
rows of teaspoon children,
each sucking a tiny silver thumb.

Milk Dreams
Watercolour on Note Page

Pocketbook Memorandum
Sketch (vi)

Christmas in July. Silver coins in husband's coat pocket.
Surprises for the children but the best waited outside for
me—a goat, blue collared & chimed.

Honeycomb sticky golden,
antlers sun-scrubbed,
barn owl feathers,
a chalk-white goat
more dog than kid.

Belle
Watercolour on Note Page

Pocketbook Memorandum
Sketch (vii)

An afternoon spent touring the countryside in pleasure & joy.

Wool lapel button-holed with orange blossom—
perfume on the coat of mister lumberjack, woodsman
road builder, factotum & father to three bundles
riding sacked as sugar on a day uncommon bright.

To Market
Watercolour on Note Page

Pocketbook Memorandum
Sketch (viii)

*I admire the independence of mice, squirrels, rabbits & men
to the unruly dependence of wild children. Did Mother know
that images split the truth in fractions?*

Boots socks laces
stockings
shirts trousers coats
leggings trample
bite suck chew
the larder lean.

Trapped
Watercolour on Note Page

In Reflection of Greater Risk Taking

i.
Dear Sister,
Breasts corseted with strips of cotton sheeting,
shirt buttoned flat. Games played after church—
when we were boys.

ii.
Irregular heartbeats, fitful games of escape—
sack races
trousers belted for jump,
yet the finish line moved
as men in beaver top-hats prized us with dresses.

iii.
I hear you, yes:
Your words are Renaissance fingers touched to my wrist,
heart, lips.
Sister-cosmographer, geographer, medic's weathered ear
pressed against the future.

iv.
Let's dress in feathers, grey-mottled, untethered.
First place in the egg & spoon race.
Last to disappear.

Poised Steady with Both Hands as the Axe
Tingles my Arms

stitches long divide my skirt into breeches
           blouse come loose at the neck
dark stains under the arms
           boots to leather my bare ankles
felled logs that roll under the weight
           of my perch as unpaid farm hand to his axe
                                                  I ask
how many trees topple in the service of house?
How many women unbalanc'd from their Orbit fly?

Waves Rise Botanical Wild

I wake inside the bones of a ship sailing amniotic
oceans, tidal pools, tears of the crocodile, my nightgown
clinging like a reputation for sin. No crying—birth is the
grit between Heave & pitch: waves crash, curse my old
carousing self overturned, head-over-heels & miscarried
to sea

      I might have named her Pearl,
      swaddled in a fisher's veil—

Poppy Garden

Heat haze,
sudden urges
& the blood-
burst of babies.

One for me,
one for he
& one for misery
born pale
as gaslight
in the gathering
dusk.

The Darkness of Wrong Counsel

I've got designs
on interior décor. I've got paint
& ladder & the faculty of Mind
to crash shelves, pictures, mirror,
flannel wool curtains.

Folds fall. Dust chokes.
Wood floors heap with blunder.

My every mistake, every wrong turn,
every miscalculation.

I ivy-climb the walls.
Balance tins & brushes.

Black—
            be the pigment of his temper,
            the absence of my glow.

I Am Lady but I Do Not Carry her Lamp

Companion is an icy Brook—my face, my head, my
bearing stunned into constant Nurse to his delirium tremens.

The fifth season in the cycle of unreason tinged
with Frost killing & thirst. My cupped hands sucked.

He sweats.
I dip & cloth his brow, wring anxious hallucinations
from a Fool's Battle in the rum trenches of bravado—

   Little Brook, Little Brook look:
Accretions of umber blood on my cheek pay homage
to his fist.

Am I criminal to coax Wolf down our chimney,
devour the crude wayfarer Slumped in sleep—?
      Little Brook, I am Everything
      but nice.

Circumstances in Regard to Endurance

Wind hymns through the gaps
in love's logic: Acts of trust take on the character of water.
Daylight shapes succumb to shadow. Tricks, bargains,
his habit of disguising failure with Rogue promises.
And the godsome air—mosquito-choked. I no longer care
who sees me vulgar spit.

I will not swallow. None of it.

Fancy Me Agent of the Out of Doors

I turn rocks with the dull point of a walking stick—
      prod the soft rot of timbers fallen.
Was a time when nothing was lost to me.
      Neither stocking, scarf, nor the look in his eyes
that fevered abnormal strains to my heart.

Such was our habit—I was Urgent Uncertainty, my own
most patient,
      quelled by the arrangement of combs,
high collar, high colour coaxed from a bit of flush pink
& flutter. He breathed promise between my skin & marrow.

In these woods I scatter ruin, dull the shine of every black
beetle that dares escape the flat heel of my boot.

My Most Patient—I poke a plunged nest & cause Inquiries,
disturb the fur-lined depths of dens.

If love be a thing lost &—
      Once a leather book-strap mapped its way home
      to me.
      Once a black button
          a white cat.

Do you suppose I am tipp'd?
Dare I find ever in his arms the dip
                & curve
of myself?

Sense of Favours Felt

I caught a glimpse of Other
dressed in ragged stuff cut low at the neck
& in great need of cleaning. She raced
a forest path so I lost her to the Rustle,
glossy leaves dark green, her odour resinous
lingered strong but in quick sight I discerned
remote allusion: two dim stars—
hazel hints of sister in the eyewink.

Pocketbook Memorandum
Sketch (ix)

*Garden plot responds to spring's weak light but my jar of yellow
ochre is empty spent.*

Faint line tender-sprung beaded romaine blushed oak iceberg
lime green bibb deep burgundy frilly French butterhead veined
with nerves.

Salad Days
Watercolour on Note Page

Pocketbook Memorandum
Sketch (x)

I've lost count of the years the way I've lost track of myself.

Horizon lines of silence
the air
between pastures old & new
wing & hoof radiant
     giddy-up
     get along little turquoise.

Time: Travel by Horse
Watercolour on Note Page

Witness at the Window (An Inclination to Believe)

Dear_____
My prayer for fond companion is satisfied in a fashion
curious
as the night study
of stars by their manifestation in a puddle—

                  Do you believe

in Sympathies? Do you   never
feel a secret intelligence which
     unites the notions of one friend with
          another? Is it possible that in the depths
            of white wilderness I am
befriended   not
by lover, traveler, pilgrim
but by Blooms   of ice on the window?
I ask: Who is their author

        by what authority do these etchings
        disclose
        that someone (you?)
        thinks of me   remembers.

The Canada sun sings tenor as I stand before the piano
of high noon
read residual signs at the porthole of Communion—
                  I am not forgotten
   yes?

We Bask for a Few Days in the Warm Sunshine of Domestic Happiness & Awake One Morning to Find a Beautiful Exceedingly

Its limp neck broken,
blood beads set as type—

My dear Queen,
        Your spirit pilots thus & falls partridge
at my threshold. I write in thanks
for your guidance to bundle the gift
in my apron skirt humble,
cradle the body across my yard
to a puddle recent fresh & mirrored
with cloud.

        My first thought was baptismal
but that be a mother's imaginings.
Instead I fixed my hands to task
& performed
a most careful examination.
Did I flinch from my Attitude? Never
once & certainly not
as your Majesty's Servant & Good Naturalist
charmed by Discovery—

        I lined the water with cloth to create
a hammock for your specimen,
bathed wing feathers, tail, white satin belly,
claws mud-caked wherein I found: three seeds,
bluish-black but not so dense as peppercorns—

I confess to feeling akin
a sort of blue stocking for in that moment
my throat desired a deep tobacco draw—
(the pinch I forbid Husband)
but I rolled & lit for my alone pleasure.

A small celebration,
a singular understanding: we are all
transported   dropped from the mouth
of a blood-dark sky.

Types & Shadows

I roam rooms inside of rooms in nightgown & bare feet,
linen clouds
ankle deep. My walk pillowed
as I sleep.

Listen—scratch of mice breeding behind walls.
I'll stuff holes with jewellers' cotton next time I pass.

Look—through yellowed cracks in the night: an entryway
inlaid with marble & the sound of a child's last game.
Coal-piece no bigger than a nub of cold star—be marker, be
leavings, be grid lines incised, the worn hop-over-scotches
ghostly white as Evening star in moonlight.

Visit—from the long gone son
whose bedtime kisses high-collared my throat.

On this Day of Days

New babe rings in the Season—
another servant
up
& Quit.

Merry—
joy—

rum-soaked, Milky letdown
foil-wrapped xmas wishes,
red-knit stockings Lumped with afterbirth—

tissue paper hats tossed pink, yellow
orange, the air inflamed
with Disorder—

gather my wincey skirts. Cross my ankles.
hold my gaze:
Ruby-throated shepherds sing
Handel's Messiah
while his lord Leaps
domestic rage
for women's work undone—

Inglenook smoke rises
behind the ancestral wing chair

passing on—
passing—

How I wish.

Sweet Yeast Dough Does a Good Cackle Make

Shall we cake?
Do let's while
babes sleep—Devil's

Food, Honey Angel,
Mock Angel, hush!
for heaven's sake.

The rise
& fall of yeast
in mattressed layers

tiered. Two lovers
kiss-kissing across
le croquembouch.

Sweet cream,
sweet delusion.
Lemon curd curdling

dreams, my soul
to keep forty winks,
one hundred years.

Sugar van Winkle,
butter, eggs, cracked
& whisked through

this night—
Moon Cake, Fairy,
Pineapple Upside

Down,
if I should die
before I wake

icing my soul
my soul to bake:
Miracle, Lady

Baltimore, Mock Pound,
Ribbon Layer
glazed confection,

piped respite
from baker's men.
Sticky fingers,

twisted bed sheets,
border of pink
fondant

infant lips
rooting pillows of flesh
overflowing.

Woman Cleaning Turnips

Pulled from earth's black bowels & issued by smells
intestinal. Servile play—shovel, sharp sticks, a rusted
spade. The children's turnip harvest hauled indoors & laid
proud at my feet like wingless offerings. In exchange
for what? That I slaughter the vegetables instead of them?
That I hold fast to character that defeats me? I play their game,
become a Chardin domestic released from the master's frame.
Sit. Take up the knife, bend & peel amidst bloated disorder.
Arrange my countenance in dialect with the idiom of laughing
idiots. Turnips they have brought me & turnips they shall eat:
baked, stewed, boiled, mashed, poked with a fork & roasted
like goose. Such enthusiasm for labours painted in tawny
copper light. Dirt-grey apron folds grained with earthly woes.
Look out, look down, look what I've become.

I Will Mount a Broken Ladder but I Will Not Surrender. I Will Not

My conceit is a square hole fixed with Glass & curtain,
an unblinking eye on the northern sky washed outside
clean, thanks to no offer of assistance from he & he & he
who smoke & jaw pamphlets, a rude triple the likesame
as these surrounds:
        black boots & rough mouths, red fingers knuckling
the bottle by its skinny neck.

I ignore the lot,
untamed talk of Canada West,
stay my heart to the season green-bursting, drag
ladder & bucket inside to rinse & polish in circles
until clouds, sky—

Idiot.

He spits laughter at my expense. Salutes
the wave of my dirty white rag.

Pocketbook Memorandum
Sketch (xi)

I call myself Artist & retreat to a private shed whose
atmosphere does brace me well. Light is good, clear-cracked.

Lank hair side-sectioned,
waved tender,
one ear veiled thus.
The other tuned
to the Gladding.

Canadian Self-portrait
Watercolour on Note Page

Pocketbook Memorandum
Sketch (xii)

Snow-drift, snow-drop, snow-balled, snow-deep, snow-crowned, snow-buried under crystals. No two alike.

Chorus of keening
from a snowman & woman,
their neckless heads leaning
into gravity's pitch,
mouths a cherry-red O.

Visitors to the New World
Pen & Ink on Note Page

I MUST NOT LET THE FIRE GROW
HYSTERICAL

Promises Federal—Acres of Plenty for Any Man
    off his Head

i.
Wind NW, hard gales & drift by afternoon.
He rides the train west with two sons
while I trample inner rooms
alone but for the youngest boy,
drag & search for signs   any
clearing, any change in the adverse—

ii.
Moderate gales SE.
I sit & desk the window at a 45° angle
of endurance.
I am under the weather, unswell.

iii.
Chimney trapped three pigeons for my Society:
one for news
        free land, no fences
one for gossip
        women are scarce
one for pie
        edges crimped & sealed (no escape)

iv.
Mouth yawned SW,
snow on the tip—
More explicit than language, yes.
Whitened prior to meaning.
I translate ink & frost
the lacking state of Wind prior to sound.
Breath, followed by a fit of tears.

I must not let the fire grow hysterical.

v.
Fingers in confession with clavicle—
trace the hollow.
Up in choke—

vi.
Winds howling NE—snow squall:
In a burst of backwoods ingenuity,
I axe the wedding chest,
kindle sparks into the flame-shapes of never need:
Sunday gloves flimsy,
satin evening bag embroidered with stars,
parcel of music rolled tight as a pine log:

how warm the chorus—
       blaze of Voices, operatic
arias crackle, light the stage & dry my weeping cotton
stockings—
Bravo!

vii.

Restless weather NW,
fire knuckling loud as gunshot. I am mattressed between
buffalo skins flattened by animal stench, fear
steaming from bloodied bowels.

viii.

Fresh gales temporal—
Journal & diarize—all days, every Gone & accounted:
visits with the King, affairs of court, household accounts,
letters unreceived, babies unborn, decades
towered like wooden trunks.

More than Winter in the Air

i.

Eyes ringed with grease & candle black—
      the rouge interlude of his lower lip. When

he I loved—
our season the after-blush: a seaside sojourn,
sun, windburn, the sight of myself in the bloodrush
to his cheeks   tall grass warmed by Heat corporeal.

Now everything once right slips wrong.
That chill.
By degrees.

ii.

blood hard & frozen spiked   carnage I spy on my hike
to never mind, never fear the in-between of sweet & Bitter,
tang of seasons nuanced as the twitch of a rabbit's nose;
where there's smoke there's terror—

iii.

View to no Warbling thrill,
  my features dry as cracknel

worsening all the while sun
enters Capricorn, bearded goat

fabled as a constellation
of cream-pots, each & every prized

with potion: bee venom, snake
venom, caviar, charcoal, essence

of algae smoothed into my every
Inkling. I am disposed for the brumal.

My countenance an assemblage
of Graces.

Am I not the palest most striking
winter-apple?

iv.

The body stripped of its integuments

my skeleton, devoid of distortion
bones entire—

no skin, flesh, vessels, nothing to support the Doctrine of
Structure:
        what holds me   here

jelly won't set   bread won't rise   breasts
dear—
        I am crystalled to the True marrow.

The Smell of Rain

i.

Boy hitched the team *hell-bent hi ho woe!*

straight for the ditch—

roman miles this side of marsh & sudden geese uprising

crisscrossed, crooned

mighty knock to the noggin, stuff strewn, trenched

& ringing pain

between the lining of my brain & skull. Ache newly

tender. He offered a son's

hand; stood me plumb least I teetered the smarting blow;

upright straight-standing;

numb as a wooden spoon. Horses dumb-whipped & blamed

to a hitching post.

ii.

Our picnic spill: black tea, biscuit crumbs, blood
crusting its marker under my best scarf.

iii.

I prayed for Horizontal ever, the quicker swift this instant.

iv.

Weather rushed the woods & gathered the laundry.
Smell of rain unpinned.

v.

Everything bleeds: August. Rabbit's last twitch. Geese at the
junction of flight & gunshot.

vi.

Cheer me, luck me, sing me, don't leave me peony pink
& bed-tabled without water.

vii.

The way back is gauzed, turbaned. Erased.

Pocketbook Memorandum
Sketch (xiii)
I found her today in the thousand-sound of crickets,
articulate vibrations forever in translation of Mother.

Behold,
the tiny copper
trumpet
held to a bellflower's ear.

Beyond the Annex of Sound
Pen & Ink on Note Page

Pocketbook Memorandum
Sketch (xiv)
Said our goodbyes, gathered the last brown eggs. Moving west
of not knowing.

Speckled hen feathers,
goat's tail-tip curl
horse hair tendrils
auburn snippets
snipped
from my best girl.

Scissors, Glue pot & Brush
Ink Wash on Note Page

One-Way Ticket

Why close my eyes?
> Because train speed is spin.

Why strangers either side up & over?
> Because the Old World.

Why eat?
> Because pickled eggs stopper the madness.

Why brake?
> Because creeks storm the track.

Why lurch & sway & rock?
> Because a blind conductor pilots the beast.

Why watercolour lakes?
> Because the artist will paint when she quiets.

Why trees for curtains?
> Because an army of pine marches sea to sea.

Why teapots in the clouds?
> Because my moods are steeping.

Why snow in summer?
> Because Canada.

Why dust?
> Because particles of faith.

Why rigid sameness?
> Because prayer-ee.

Why freight sheds?
    Because loads burden heavy transport.
Why tall as cathedrals?
    Because elevators holy the grain.
Why men?
    Because once they were trees.
Why loading platform?
    Because my first step.
Why his arms extend the horizon?
    Because I promised.

The Oxen Dialogues

Fragments of a Journey from Prairie Train Station to Homestead

Oxen yoked to a wagon:

OXEN ONE (adult male, reddish-brown)

OXEN TWO (adult male, black)

i) Mile Unknown

OXEN ONE: Lines.

OXEN TWO: Weary-worn.

OXEN ONE: Parallel, vertical, horizontal.

OXEN TWO: Angular, diagonal, jagged.

OXEN ONE: Infinite, straight.

OXEN TWO: Continuous points collected.

OXEN ONE: Two distinct end-points.

OXEN TWO: Lines of desire?

(long beat)

OXEN ONE: Him & her.

OXEN TWO: Dumb beast.

ii) Mile Unknown

OXEN ONE: Less wealthy.

OXEN TWO: Industrious but failed.

OXEN ONE: Hill ahead. More promises.

OXEN TWO: Will she topple this rutted line?

OXEN ONE: Green gall, may three-pence purpose
and one means.

OXEN TWO: That a town?

OXEN ONE: Telegraph polls.

OXEN TWO: Whoa there, brother.

(long beat)

OXEN ONE: Gossip unseats her.

OXEN TWO: After years, house was all.

OXEN ONE: Twice plants and love's waves.

OXEN TWO: Few over-dense.

OXEN ONE: Ah, but duty & poverty.

OXEN TWO: Independence.

OXEN ONE: Still, gun-cold & cheers.

OXEN TWO: Shoulder to occurrence.

OXEN ONE: Shoreline tugs my brute conscience.

iii) Mile Unknown

OXEN ONE: Gum-leather.

OXEN TWO: At the war office?

OXEN ONE: Like rats in a granary.

OXEN TWO: Iron chain, cedar-crowned.

OXEN ONE: Look, harebells.

OXEN TWO: In godly clusters. Will he notice & pause for her?

(long beat)

OXEN ONE: He's map & paper west.

OXEN TWO: Vermillion pummeling lines by-and-by.

OXEN ONE: Meaning?

OXEN TWO: Gone justice!

iv) Mile Unknown

OXEN TWO: Swamp-alder. Smell the air.

OXEN ONE: She'll pine for sun this day.

OXEN TWO: Stars but cried, stupefied.

OXEN ONE: Fate be thin phrenology.

OXEN TWO: We measure well.

OXEN ONE: Imagine unconfinement to the line.

OXEN TWO: Hoped-for comfort.

OXEN ONE: Should one of us not angle for mercies?

OXEN TWO: Heave the toss'd rise, then rest.

v) Mile Unknown

OXEN ONE: Such nights as these.

(long beat)

OXEN TWO: Mosquitoes, bears, wolf lumbering.

OXEN ONE: Her wet cheek pressed close my flank is rose
            to muscled feel.

OXEN TWO: Smitten. There's a mistake.

OXEN ONE: Yoked.

OXEN TWO: Ah.

OXEN ONE: Stay the line.

OXEN TWO: Stay the straight curve.

vi) Mile Unknown

OXEN TWO: Large paus'd bush farm journey this.

OXEN ONE: On spirit.

OXEN TWO: On mercy, second sight.

OXEN ONE: Brush white absence.

OXEN TWO: Blind sky.

OXEN ONE: Eyes past flame.

OXEN TWO: No wonder she wings. All friends.

OXEN ONE: While face?

OXEN TWO: Road.

OXEN ONE: Gully.

OXEN TWO: Crushing grey.

OXEN ONE: Woe this passage, mine.

OXEN TWO: Theirs.

OXEN ONE: Drink shade.

vii) Mile Unknown

OXEN ONE: But for children.

OXEN TWO: I suppose.

OXEN ONE: Fair hair floating in the wind.

OXEN TWO: Washing the shore.

OXEN ONE: Agreed.

OXEN TWO: Nothing escapes you.

OXEN ONE: Her hands braid.

OXEN TWO: Constant.

OXEN ONE: Heaven, you suppose?

(beat)

OXEN TWO: At which mile?

OXEN TWO: The same genius who invented blame.

OXEN ONE: I know not.

OXEN TWO: Every dish broken.

OXEN ONE: Not a tear.

OXEN TWO: She be hardened.

OXEN ONE: She reads me like a harmony extract.

OXEN TWO: And I, you. Ready?

OXEN ONE: Mud on crockery.

OXEN TWO: Pincherry juice on crockery.

OXEN ONE: Squirrel blood on crockery.

OXEN TWO: Crab apple jelly on crockery.

OXEN ONE: Hog's lard on crockery.

OXEN TWO: Listen to us, talking like artists.

OXEN ONE: She lines the way.

OXEN TWO: Ah, but he whips the air until sky cracks
          lightning.

OXEN ONE: You reduce me to poetry.

OXEN TWO: How now my brown cow?

OXEN ONE: These rains, her dry eyes.

ix) Mile Unknown

OXEN TWO: She's all-overish.

OXEN ONE: Morning sickness?

OXEN TWO: Fimble-famble. You're off your chump.

OXEN ONE: My smeller's true.

OXEN TWO: You sniff the piss she makes?

OXEN ONE: Crude beast I am.

OXEN TWO: Astute.

OXEN ONE: He's better for the absence of heavy-wet.

OXEN TWO: And she more honour-bright.

x) Mile Unknown

OXEN ONE: I've not a blinker since the mud.

OXEN TWO: Hail be the prairie's fist.

xi) Mile Unknown

OXEN TWO: Sparsely wooded.

OXEN ONE: A grove of spruce to the north.

OXEN TWO: I'm all bellows to mend and ready drop.

OXEN ONE: I've a mind to don a bonnet.

OXEN TWO: I've not the breath to snort.

OXEN ONE: She's low to rocks with shovel.

OXEN TWO: Him with crowbar at the stumps.

OXEN ONE: Not us, my friend.

OXEN TWO: Not us.

xii) Mile Known: End of the Line

OXEN ONE: Bones.

OXEN TWO: For now shall I sleep in the dust.

Artist Unknown

towel
nail
tree

Ablution
Oils on cracked porcelain basin
Artist unknown

light pools
in the coulee cleft
hillocks
broken slopes
yellow-brushed
eye sweeping
the horizon bone

Wedding Gift for Last Son
Oils on canvas
Artist unknown

dawn mist
conversation
in a creek bed
poplars telegraphing
prismatic
verdant tattle

Awake
Oils on chipped mug
Artist unknown

indigo bleeds
the edge of remote
so vast
loneliness
doubles in pain
drops its stone
bends at the knees

Sky
Oils on cracked china saucer
Artist unknown

thick-brushed & knife-stroked quick
wolf willow
hued mute & hunched cleft-deep
luminous greenshot
alpha-grey

Predator
Oils on fractured porcelain vase
Artist unknown

tin wash basin
shovel-scooped
with snow
for tea water
set to kettle
steam plumes
sheep tails
mare's tails
herding
a thunder head

Shadows
Oils on chipped bowl
Artist unknown

snowdrifts windward-skirted
against wheat sheaves tall as a dance

partner blue shadows long cast
silkbolts frost-shot music in the downbeat

ghosts waltz along the crest
white arms raised to the moonless

Winter
Oils on glass creamer fragment
Artist unknown

oats soaked in water scalding
stovetop watched least the slop boil—
        salt-pinch
milk-stream
honey syrup fig-chop
breakfast spooned at midnight
moon balanced on the tongue tip
lip-smacked & swallowed

Steeped
Oils on blue crockery tea cup (no handle)
Artist unknown

steam spools from coffee cup lip
violet-blue harebells clutched in a jam jar
tablecloth   afternoon breeze lifting
                                    the hem

Another Woman's Voice
Oils on chipped gravy boat
Artist unknown

horizon divides
those who forget
from those who remember
the suckling child
swaddled & buried
under tricks to ease
the dumb leaving

rich distance
blood rinsed in chalky light

Broken Heart
Watercolour on cracked mug
Artist unknown

choir of voices raise
the night sky
as stars
sing the song
first heard
in the purpling
womb

Sky Sketch
Oils on cracked spooner
Artist unknown

small pond frozen in the grace
between winter & kill
ice hugged tight to the land
last breath
the beckoning gesture

The Emphatic Claim
Oils on notched dinner plate
Artist unknown

flat spaces flat
tablet
the peneplain interrupted by the level
ring of horizon   gutted
light glareless
transparent
pale face
hatless head
of a woman

Interior Landscape
Oils on cracked soup bowl
Artist unknown

Sources

Where from language, ideas, the poem's gesture?

This collection began soon after the death of my mother in 2011. I felt the attention of what I can only describe as a presence during the early days of my grief. I didn't feel frightened, nor did I feel consoled. What I felt was curiosity because my writing took on a mannered voice that lifted me from my sorrow and into something that felt like ancient sadness.

I began to wonder how our foremothers and their daughters said goodbye in the Old World *knowing* they would never see, touch, or hear one another again. There would have been letters, of course, and eventually trains, but no email, no telephone, no Skype, no Boeing aircraft, and probably no time or money for a cross-Atlantic visit by ship. Most settlers would not have attended their mother's funeral.

Yet the voice of the poems seemed to insist that communication was not only possible, but necessary and eternal. I wondered who the messengers might have been in those days. The wind? A crow's call? A river's white water? Yes, yes, and yes.

So I began to read, guided by a brief family history: immigration to southern Ontario from England and Ireland in the early 1800s; my own interprovincial migration in 1982 when I moved to Saskatoon from Hamilton (with a four-year stop in Regina). The following works (read either in part or in whole) suggested the arc of *Never Mind*:

Ballstadt, Carl, Elizabeth Hopkins, and Michael Peterman. *Susanna Moodie, Letters of a Lifetime.* (Toronto: University of Toronto Press, 1985).

Burkhardt, Frederick. *Origins—Selected Letters of Charles Darwin 1822–1859*, with an introduction by Stephen Jay Gould. (Cambridge: Cambridge University Press, 2008).

Creighton, Donald. *The Story of Canada*. (Toronto: Macmillan, 1959).

Gwyn, Richard. *Nation Maker: Sir John A Macdonald, His Life, Our Times*. (Toronto: Random House of Canada, 2012).

Matthews, S. Leigh. *Looking Back—Canadian Women's Prairie Memoirs and Intersections of Culture, History, and Identity*. (Calgary: University of Calgary Press, 2010).

Moodie, Susanna. *Roughing It in the Bush; Or, Life in Canada* Volumes 1 & 2. (Toronto: McClelland & Stewart, 1923).

Saul, John Ralston. *A Fair Country, Telling Truths About Canada*. (Toronto: Penguin Canada, 2009).

Waiser, Bill. *Saskatchewan—A New History*. (Calgary: Fifth House Limited, 2005).

White, Donny. *In Search of Geraldine Moodie*. (Regina: Canadian Plains Research Centre, University of Regina, 1998).

Form, line, and Nerve were prompted by many of the works of Sylvia Plath, C.D. Wright, Emily Dickinson, W.B. Yeats, Jane Austen, Lucie Brock-Broido, and e.e. cummings.

Notes on the Poems

In "The Swell & Pitch of the Surging Grief" the phrase, "sine qua non," is Latin for an essential or necessary condition.

In "Slumber Clos'd Her Silver-Streaming Eyes"—the title is borrowed from Homer's epic poem, *The Odyssey*, (Book XXI).

In "The Days are Brief & Pale, the Nights Deep Lakes Dark"—the title is borrowed from Rachel Cusk's, *A Life's Work*, (p. 38). Also the line, "bruised bank of cloud," is from the same book, (p. 55).

"We Bask for a Few Days in the Warm Sunshine of Domestic Happiness & Awake One Morning to Find a Beautiful Exceedingly" was prompted by a line that Charles Darwin wrote in a letter to his uncle: "I am dying by inches, from not having anybody to talk to about insects."

The last line in the poem, "Poised Steady with Both Hands as the Axe Tingles my Arms," is a corrupt version of Alexander Pope's glorious line, "Let earth unbalanc'd from her orbit fly" (from *Essay on Man*). This line also introduces Section I.

"Keepsake of Affection Pinned Miniature Close" was prompted by the exhibition produced by Library and Archives Canada and shown at the Mendel Art Gallery, Saskatoon, SK in 2013 and titled, *I Know You by Heart, Portrait Miniatures*.

"The Smell of Rain" was prompted by W.B. Yeats's poem, "A Prayer for My Daughter."

"Woman Cleaning Turnips" is the title of a painting by Jean-Baptiste-Siméon Chardin.

"More Than Winter in the Air," pulls language from the 1828 definition of anatomy found in Noah Webster's *Dictionary of the English Language*. Additionally, the line "he I loved," was sourced from Wordsworth's poem "Lucy," specifically, "When she I loved look'd every day."

The language in "The Oxen Dialogue" draws from two sources: "Variants in Copy-text (the Rejected Variant)" found in

Roughing It in the Bush; Or, Life in Canada by Susanna Moodie. Edited by Ballstadt et al. And in "Mile Unknown (vi)", some of the words come from "The Art of Manliness—Manly Slang from the Nineteenth Century" (www.art of manliness.com): accessed November, 2015. The closing line in "Mile Known (x)," "For now shall I sleep in the dust," is from the *The King James Bible* (Job 7).

In "Pocketbook Memorandum sketch (viii)" "images split the truth in fractions" is from "A Sequence" by Denise Levertov, found in *The Jacob's Ladder*.

The ekphrastic poem titled "Interior Landscape" was prompted by the novel *Wolf Willow* by Wallace Stegner. Specifically, "flat spaces flat/ tablet/ the peneplain interrupted by the level."

Acknowledgements

Thank you to the Canada Council for the Arts and to the Saskatchewan Arts Board for invaluable support.

Thanks to CBC Radio One, SoundXChange, and producer Kelley Jo Burke for airing a series of poems from this collection. An earlier version of "We Bask for a Few Days in the Warm Sunshine of Domestic Happiness & Awake One Morning to Find a Beautiful Exceedingly" appeared in *Grain Magazine*, Vol. 42.4. Several of the poems were long-listed in the 2014 CBC Poetry competition.

I am grateful for the illustration by Soul Reverie artist Catrin Welz-Stein; her brush led me down through the centuries and helped me to visualize the woman in these poems.

Big thanks to my tribe. Good friends read and listened to these poems over the course of many years. Their suggestions made the poems better. I thank The Regina Combine: Byrna Barclay, Robert Currie, Judith Krause, Jim McLean, Bruce Rice, Paul Wilson, for their kindness and wisdom.

I thank poet Jennifer Still for lending her spark to this collection. Her work helped me to balance the level.

Thank you to the 2013 Sage Hill Writing Experience poetry colloquium, particularly the generosity and encouragement of Ken Babstock, Kristina Bresnen, Heidi Greco, Joanna Lilley, and Mitch Spray.

Thanks to Gerry Hill, Steven Ross Smith, Patricia Young and everyone at Turnstone Press. Warmest thanks to my editor, Alice Major, for astute observation and insight.

Ongoing thanks to all those with whom I hike, bike, paddle, ski, walk river trails, sip black tea, and drink good wine. Laughter, bring it on!

Special thanks to Theresa Labreche.

Finally, heartfelt thanks to those who populate my true north—Randy and our daughters Rachel and Anna, my sister Barbara Almas, our stepmother Sara Lawrence, and my extended Burton family. Deepest thanks to the entire clan for your steady faith and your love.

Never Mind is **Katherine Lawrence's** third collection of poetry. The manuscript won the 2015 John V. Hicks Long Manuscript Award and the 2014 City of Regina Writing Award. Her previous collections have been equally honoured. Originally from Hamilton, Ontario, Katherine chairs Access Copyright Foundation, and is a former president of the Sage Hill Writing Experience board of directors. She moved to Saskatchewan in 1982 and currently lives in Saskatoon with her husband.